Jamestown, Virginia

Jamestown, Virginia

Dennis Brindell Fradin

Marshall Cavendish
Benchmark

New York

Marshall Cavendish Benchmark
99 White Plains Road
Tarrytown, NY 10591
www.marshallcavendish.us

Text and map copyright © 2007 by Marshall Cavendish Corporation
Map by XNR Productions

All Internet sites were available and accurate when sent to press.

Library of Congress Cataloging-in-Publication Data

Fradin, Dennis B.
Jamestown, Virginia / by Dennis Brindell Fradin.
p. cm. — (Turning points of United States history)
Includes bibliographical references and index.
ISBN-13: 978-0-7614-2122-1
ISBN-10: 0-7614-2122-X
1. Jamestown (Va.)—History—17th century—Juvenile literature. 2. Virginia—History—Colonial period, ca. 1600-1775—Juvenile literature.
I. Title II. Series: Fradin, Dennis B. Turning points of United States history.
F234.J3F73 2006
975.5'425102—dc22
2005016018

Photo Research by Connie Gardner

Cover: Settlers roll barrels of tobacco onto a ship for export.

Cover Photo: Hulton Archive/Getty Images
Title Page: Richard T. Nowitz/CORBIS
The photographs in this book are used by permission and through the courtesy of: *Corbis*: Bettmann, 6, 12, 18, 38; *Art Resource*: Bildarchiv Preussischer
Kulturbesitz, 8; HIP/Scala, 9, 20; New York Public Library, 27; *The Granger Collection*: 10, 11, 14, 16, 19, 22, 28, 33, 36; *North Wind Picture Archives*: 24;
Brown Brothers: 26; *Getty Images*: Hulton Archives, 30, 34, 42-43.

Editorial Director: Michelle Bisson
Art Director: Anahid Hamparian
Printed in China
1 3 5 6 4 2

Contents

This illustration depicts Leif Eriksson and his crew off the coast of Vineland.

Exploration and Early Colonization of America

The identity of the first non-Indian explorer to reach what is now the United States remains a mystery.

Centuries ago, African people apparently reached the New World by canoe. Around the year 1000, the Viking Leif Eriksson landed in an unknown part of North America. The Vikings were from Norway and nearby regions. Amerigo Vespucci, an Italian, may have reached what is now the United States on a voyage said to have been made in 1497 to 1498. North and South America were named for Amerigo. In the late 1400s John Cabot, sailing for England, visited Canada and perhaps the present-day United States. Spanish **explorer** Ponce de Leon arrived in Florida in 1513.

This painting by Theodore de Bry (1528–1598) is called "Amerigo Vespucci Surrounded by Sea Monsters on his Way to the New World."

By the 1500s and 1600s, several countries wanted to build settlements in what is now the United States. They included France, Spain, England, and the Netherlands.

8

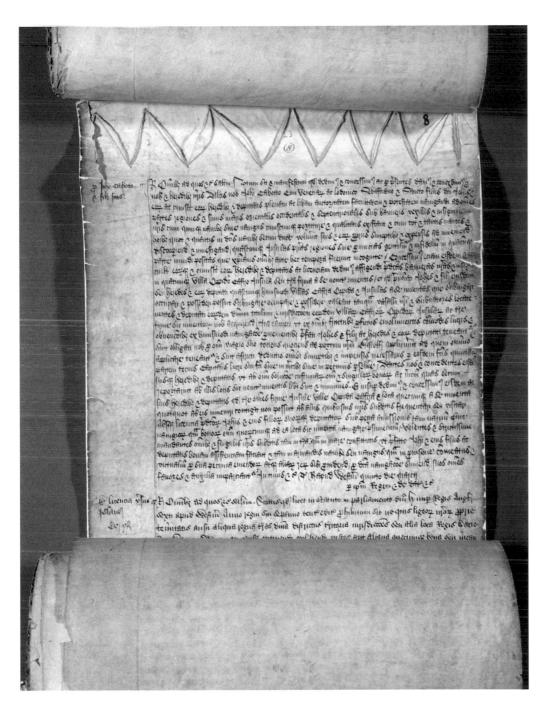

In March 1496, King
Henry VII issued
these letters allowing
John Cabot to
explore unknown
lands for Britain.

FLORIDA

IV CENTENARIO DE

80 CTS

PONCE DE LEÓN

CORREOS

ESPAÑA

Spanish explorer Juan Ponce de Leon is shown on a Spanish postage stamp, 1960.

In 1562, twenty-six Frenchmen built a settlement called Charlesfort along what is now the South Carolina coast. They neglected to plant crops and might have starved if not for friendly Native Americans. Adding to their problems, the leader of the **colony** was a **tyrant**. He hanged one colonist for saying something that annoyed him, and banished another to a deserted island. The Frenchmen **abandoned** Charlesfort after a year. A short time later, in 1564, the French tried again. They built Fort Caroline near what is now Jacksonville, Florida, but it did not last, either.

F. Maij

This colored engraving by Theodore de Bry was made in 1591. It shows the beginning of the construction of Fort Caroline on an island in the St. Johns River in 1564.

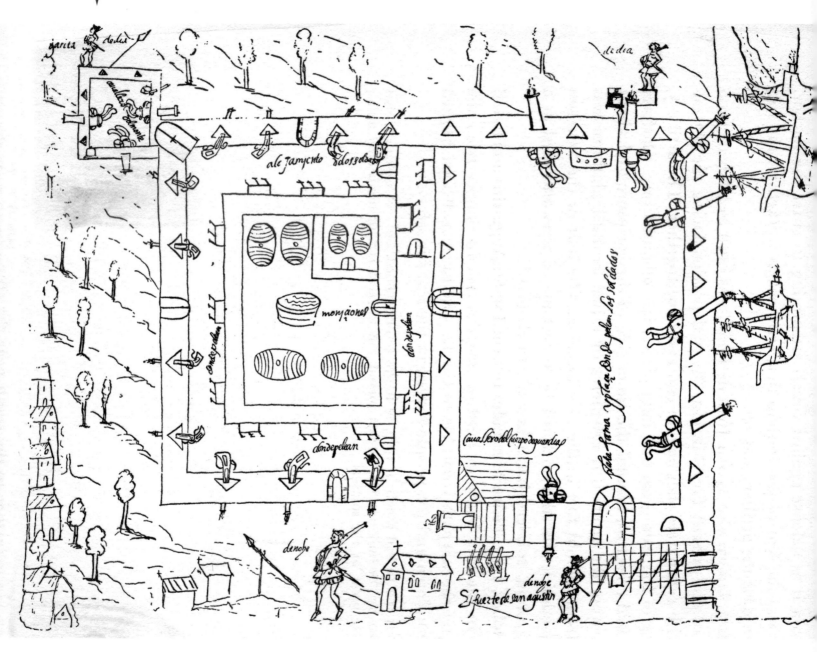

This illustration shows the plan for the fort at St. Augustine, Florida (1565–1566) built by Don Pedro Menendez de Aviles. The original sixteenth-century sketch was drawn from memory.

Spain, which by 1550 had **conquered** Mexico and much of South America, also wanted to rule what is now the United States. In 1565 Spaniards captured the French Fort Caroline, and began a settlement of their own nearby. Called St. Augustine, Florida, this Spanish settlement was there to stay. Today it has the honor of being the oldest European-built town in the United States. Spain then began more settlements in what are now several states.

This painting shows the founding of the English colony at Roanoke Island in 1587.

England Steps In

England got off to a later start than France and Spain in its quest to colonize America.

The first attempt came in 1585 when Englishmen sent by Sir Walter Raleigh began the "City of Raleigh" on North Carolina's Roanoke Island. A food shortage and other problems led the men to give up and depart for England in the middle of the year 1586. Had they stayed a little longer, the City of Raleigh might have become England's first permanent American colony. A supply ship sent by Sir Walter Raleigh arrived shortly after the settlement was abandoned.

This colored engraving from the nineteenth century depicts John White's discovery of the deserted colony of Roanoke in 1590.

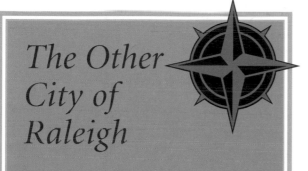

The Other City of Raleigh

Sir Walter Raleigh was a renowned English explorer, soldier, and poet. The "City of Raleigh" that he founded in 1585 had nothing to do with the city of Raleigh, North Carolina, begun two centuries later, more than 150 miles to the west.

In 1587 Sir Walter sent more settlers, this time **recruiting** families. The more than one hundred settlers who sailed to America included John White, who was to govern the colony, his daughter, Eleanor White Dare, and her husband, Ananias Dare. The **colonists** landed at Roanoke Island in July 1587 and began building homes. On August 18, 1587, Eleanor Dare gave birth to the first English child born in America, a girl named Virginia Dare.

Nine days after Virginia Dare's birth, Governor White sailed for England to get supplies. When he returned to America three years later in 1590, the colonists had vanished. They may have been killed by Native Americans, or gone to live with them. Because their fate is a mystery, the settlers who disappeared are known as the "Lost Colony."

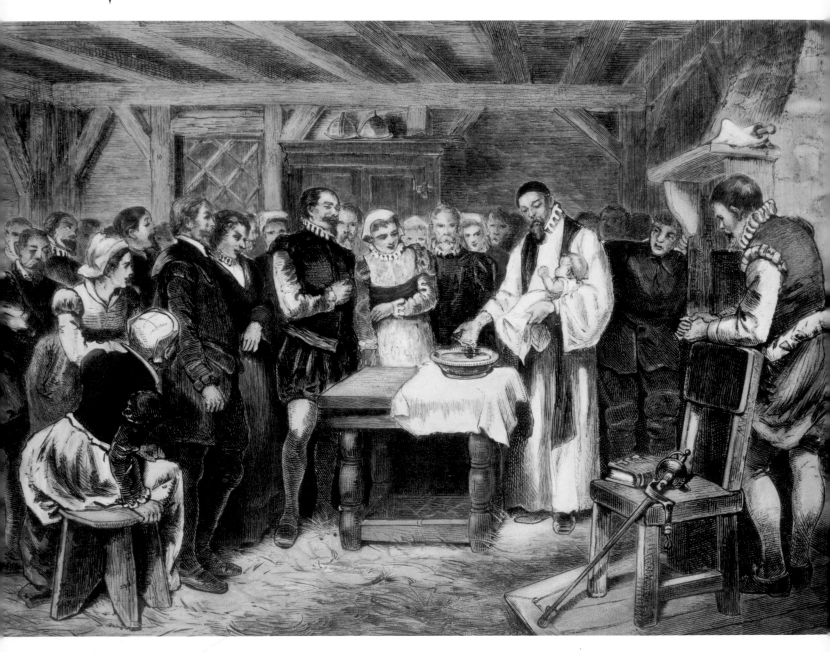

This illustration shows the birth of Virginia Dare, the first baby born to English parents in the New World.

An Indian massacre was one reason offered to explain the disappearance of what became known as the Lost Colony of Roanoke.

Other English colonies also failed. In 1602 explorer Bartholomew Gosnold sailed with about thirty men to what is now the northeastern corner of the United States. Gosnold and his men planted crops and began a tiny settlement at what is now Massachusetts' Cuttyhunk Island, but it proved to be just temporary.

Captain Gosnold trades with the Native Americans in Virginia in 1634 in this engraving by Theodore de Bry. Gosnold holds a knife, arrow, necklace, and feather in his hands. In the background are Indian canoes and European ships.

Another English attempt came in 1607 when a group of settlers began the Popham Colony in Maine. They built homes and storehouses as well as the first English ship constructed in North America. As a result of a bitter winter and other difficulties, the settlers returned to England after just one year.

The building of the Jamestown settlement is shown in this nineteenth century engraving.

CHAPTER THREE

The Founding of Jamestown

It was starting to look like England might never gain a foothold in America. But around the time the Popham Colony was begun, the English attempted to start another colony. In late 1606, ships named the *Susan Constant*, the *Godspeed*, and the *Discovery* left England, bound for present-day Virginia. Among the Englishmen on board was the captain of the *Godspeed*, Bartholomew Gosnold, who still wanted to settle America. Another of the **approximately** one hundred settlers was a soldier named John Smith.

A difficult four-month voyage brought the three ships to Chesapeake Bay on April 26, 1607, by the calendar then in use. The ships sailed sixty miles up a river that the Englishmen named the James River for their king, James I of England.

John Smith's Adventures

John Smith led an adventurous life. As a young man, he served as a soldier in Europe. Wounded in battle, he was taken to Turkey as a slave but killed his master, escaped, and returned to England.

Later, in Virginia, Smith had several brushes with death besides the episode that led to his rescue by Pocahontas. One incident took place while he was fishing in Chesapeake Bay, when a stingray whipped its poisonous tail into his wrist. Captain Smith survived. The place where this occurred is still called Stingray Point.

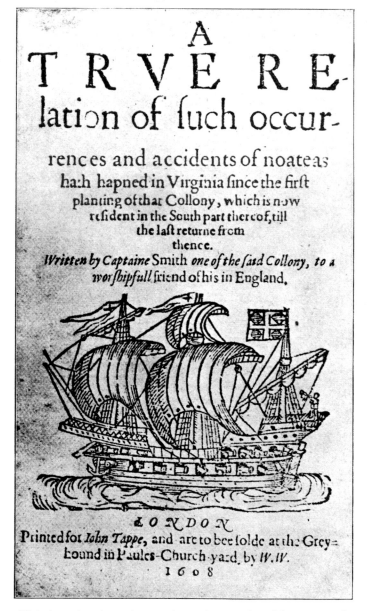

This hand-colored woodcut shows the title page of John Smith's book on his travels, written in 1608.

On May 14, 1607, the colonists landed on a **peninsula** on the north side of the river. They walked onto the shore and decided that here they would build their settlement—Jamestown—also named for their king.

The Englishmen had sailed to Virginia for various reasons. Some wanted land, which would have been difficult for them to obtain in England. Some hoped to find gold and other treasures. Some wanted to convert the American Indians to Christianity. And some came just for the sake of adventure.

It quickly became apparent that Captain John Smith was the man best able to help the colony survive. Under his direction, the men built a fort and thatch-roofed houses. But the Englishmen had arrived too late to plant food crops. Hunger soon set in.

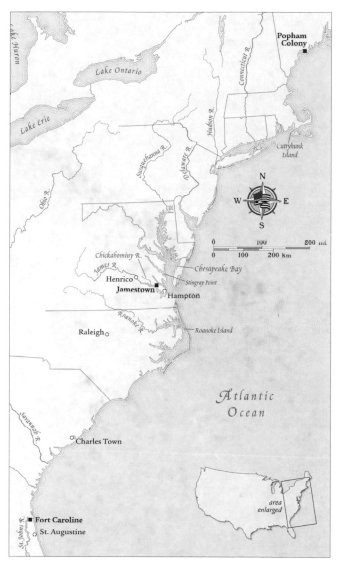

Jamestown and the Other Early Virginia Settlements

25

The Jamestown settlers almost starved to death. They were saved by the Native Americans who lived in the area.

To make things worse, the **marshes** near Jamestown were a breeding ground for mosquitoes, and the colonists' drinking water was **polluted**. By the end of the first summer at Jamestown, nearly half the settlers had died, including Captain Bartholomew Gosnold. Many of the **survivors** were very ill.

Now and then the Powhatan Indians in the region visited the settlers and traded corn and meat to them in exchange for copper and trinkets. The Englishmen couldn't get enough food this way, though, so Smith led **expeditions** to obtain more. With a few men, Smith would enter a village and trade mirrors, beads, and other items to the Native Americans for bread, corn, and deer meat. These expeditions were risky for Smith and his companions. Over the years, the Indians had been mistreated by European explorers, so they were suspicious of the Englishmen.

During the winter of 1607 to 1608, Smith and his companions were seeking food and exploring the Chickahominy River when Powhatan Indians attacked them. Smith was seized and taken to the village of Chief Powhatan (who had the same name as the tribe). At one point during a feast, Smith was forced to the ground. Several braves raised their clubs, apparently intending "to beat out [Smith's] brains," as Smith later wrote. But at the last moment the chief's daughter, Pocahontas, ran up to Smith to shield him from the blows.

This painting shows Captain John Smith after he had been rescued by the Native American princess, Pocahontas.

"Pocahontas the King's dearest daughter," wrote the captain, "got [Smith's] head in her arms, and laid her own upon his to save him from death; whereat the Emperor was contented he should live."

John Smith believed that Pocahontas, who was only about twelve years old at the time, saved his life on impulse. Many historians think that

The Baptism of Pocahontas in Jamestown, Virginia, 1613, is depicted in this oil painting by John G. Chapman.

28

The Life of Pocahontas

After saving John Smith's life, Pocahontas often visited Jamestown. She challenged the Englishmen to running contests, and taught them American-Indian words. In 1614, Pocahontas married John Rolfe, an English settler. Two years later, Pocahontas, her husband, and their young son Thomas went to England. Sadly, in March of 1617, just as the Rolfes were about to sail back to Virginia, Pocahontas died. Her son, Thomas Rolfe, was educated in England and returned to Virginia at the age of twenty.

the Indians had already decided to spare Smith, and staged this scene to symbolize Smith's "adoption" by Powhatan. The English captain and Powhatan exchanged pledges of friendship and Smith returned to Jamestown.

Powhatan's aid proved vital to the survival of the colony, where by early 1608 only thirty-eight of the original one hundred settlers remained alive. True to his pledge, Powhatan traded food to the settlers, helping Jamestown survive.

Hunger, disease, and cold killed hundreds of colonists. When they ran out of food, the colonists ate their horses, dogs, and cats. Eventually they ate rats, snakes, and even dead human bodies.

In the spring of 1610 two small ships carrying more than one hundred people docked at Jamestown. Among them was Sir Thomas Gates, who had been sent out to be Jamestown's acting governor. Jamestown's survivors begged Gates to take them in his ships to Newfoundland, Canada. There they expected to find a fishing fleet that would bring them back to England.

Sir Thomas Gates

Sir Thomas Gates and the other newcomers had lived through some **perilous** events. A year earlier they had been sailing to Virginia when their ship was wrecked in the Bermuda Islands. The **castaways** survived and built two new ships, the *Patience* and the *Deliverance*, in which they finally arrived at Jamestown in the spring of 1610. Besides Sir Thomas Gates, the new arrivals included John Rolfe, who would later marry Pocahontas.

The marriage of Pocahontas and John Rolfe in April 1614 is shown in this nineteenth century lithograph.

Gates tried without success to convince them to remain in Jamestown. Finally, he agreed to their request. It appeared that, like the "City of Raleigh," the "Lost Colony," Bartholomew Gosnold's tiny Cuttyhunk settlement, and the Popham Colony, Jamestown was going to pass out of existence.

After a winter of famine and disease, the Jamestown settlers were thrilled to see ships arriving full of supplies and more settlers.

CHAPTER FIVE

A Stroke of Luck

On a June day in 1610 the people of Jamestown packed their belongings. To the beating of a drum, they boarded at least three small ships. They sailed down the James River, leaving their little colony after three years of struggle.

No one knew it at the time, but this was a crossroads in American history. If the British had abandoned the attempt to colonize America, France, which had begun settling Canada, might swoop down from the north and become America's main colonizer. Or Spain, which had conquered much of the New World, might come up from the south. A few years into the future, in 1624, the Netherlands would begin its New Netherland territory, which would include parts of what are now New York, New Jersey, Connecticut, and Delaware.

Delaware

Several places were later named for Lord Delaware, including Delaware Bay, the Delaware River, and the colony and later state of Delaware.

Perhaps the Dutch (people from the Netherlands) would have taken over the whole East **Coast**.

But as the departing ships approached Chesapeake Bay, something remarkable occurred. The colonists spotted a small boat. The men on this boat explained that English ships carrying supplies were about to arrive. Sir Thomas Gates

A representation of the House of Burgesses in 1619 is shown in this 1833 engraving.

turned his vessels back and returned to Jamestown. The settlement had been saved in the nick of time.

The fleet that saved Jamestown was commanded by Thomas West, whose title was Lord Delaware. The colony's first official governor, Lord Delaware had brought food as well as 150 new colonists with him. Lord Delaware got the colonists to rebuild and clean up Jamestown. The Virginia Colony expanded as new settlements were begun: Hampton in 1610, Henrico in 1611, and other towns soon after. In 1619, Virginia's House of Burgesses, the first lawmaking body in America composed of elected representatives, first met in Jamestown. By 1620, the Virginia Colony was home to about 2,000 colonists and was continuing to grow.

This 1856 illustration shows the signing of the Declaration of Independence.

CHAPTER SIX

The Jamestown Legacy

Jamestown helped the United States come into being. The success of Jamestown and the Virginia Colony inspired England to settle and take control of other parts of America. Eventually England ruled thirteen American colonies. Besides Virginia, they were Massachusetts, New Hampshire, New York, Connecticut, Maryland, Rhode Island, Delaware, Pennsylvania, North Carolina, New Jersey, South Carolina, and Georgia.

In 1776, the colonies announced that they had become a new nation. So in 2007 when people gather at Jamestown, they won't just be celebrating the four-hundredth birthday of England's first **permanent** American town. They will be honoring the town from which a nation grew.

Glossary

abandon—Leave.

approximately—Roughly, or about.

castaways—People who reach shore from a shipwreck.

century—A period of one hundred years.

coast—The land along a large body of water.

colonists—People who leave their country to live in a new land.

colony—A settlement built by a country beyond its borders.

conquer—To take over by force.

expeditions—Long journeys or trips.

explorer—A person who visits and studies unknown lands.

marsh—A kind of wetland.

peninsula—A piece of land that is surrounded by water on three sides.

perilous—Dangerous.

permanent—Lasting.

polluted—Dirty or impure.

recruiting—The act of arranging for people to join a group or go on a mission.

survivors—People who have remained alive through difficulties.

tyrant—A leader who is unjust.

Timeline

1000—Viking explorer Leif Eriksson lands in an unknown part of North America at about this time

1497–1498—Italian-born Amerigo Vespucci may have reached what is now the United States during one of his voyages

1490s—John Cabot, sailing for England, visits Canada and perhaps what is now the United States

1513—Spanish explorer Ponce de Leon arrives in Florida

1562—The French build the Charlesfort settlement in what is now South Carolina

1564—French build Fort Caroline in what is now Florida

1565—Spaniards begin St. Augustine, Florida, now the oldest European-built town in the United States

1585–1586—English begin and abandon "City of Raleigh" in North Carolina

1000   *1513*   *1565*

1587—English found what becomes known as the "Lost Colony" because of the settlers' disappearance

1607—Approximately one hundred Englishmen begin Jamestown, which becomes the first permanent English settlement in what is now the United States

1609–1610—"The starving time" of the Jamestown settlement

1610—Jamestown survivors nearly leave, but Lord Delaware arrives with supplies in the nick of time

1611—Settlements of Hampton and Henrico are founded

1619—Virginia's House of Burgesses, the first elected legislature in America, meets in Jamestown

1620—Virginia Colony's population reaches about 2,000

1776—Thirteen colonies declare their independence from Great Britain

2007—Happy four-hundredth birthday, Jamestown!

1607   *1619*   *2007*

Further Information

B O O K S

Collier, Christopher, and James Lincoln Collier. *The Paradox of Jamestown: 1585–1700*. New York: Benchmark Books, 1998.

Knowlton, MaryLee, and Janet Riehecky. *The Settling of Jamestown*. Milwaukee, WI: Gareth Stevens, 2002.

Marcovitz, Hal. *John Smith: Explorer and Colonial Leader*. Philadelphia: Chelsea House, 2002.

Sewall, Marcia. *James Towne: Struggle for Survival*. New York: Atheneum, 2001.

WEB SITES

A Web site with many fascinating links about the history of Jamestown
www.apva.org/history

The home page of Colonial National Historical Park
nps.gov/colo

The home page of Jamestown Settlement
www.historyisfun.org

HISTORIC SITE

Seeing the Ruins of Jamestown

Today, almost no one lives in Jamestown. But at nearby Colonial National Historical Park visitors can see ruins of the original Jamestown. Another local attraction, called Jamestown Settlement, features replicas of the fort, the first three ships, and an Indian village.

Bibliography

Billings, Warren M., John E. Selby, and Thad W. Tate. *Colonial Virginia: A History.* White Plains, NY: KTO Press, 1986.

Bridenbaugh, Carl. *Jamestown: 1544–1699.* New York: Oxford University Press, 1980.

Forman, Henry Chandlee. *Jamestown and St. Mary's: Buried Cities of Romance.* Baltimore: The Johns Hopkins Press, 1938.

Smith, John. *Captain John Smith's America: Selections From His Writings*, ed. John Lankford. New York: Harper, 1967.

Yonge, Samuel H. *The Site of Old "James Towne": 1607–1698.* Richmond, VA: The Hermitage Press, 1907.

Index

Page numbers in **boldface** are illustrations.

About the Author

Dennis Fradin is the author of 150 books, some of them written with his wife, Judith Bloom Fradin. Their recent book for Clarion, *The Power of One: Daisy Bates and the Little Rock Nine*, was named a Golden Kite Honor Book. Another of Dennis's recent books is *Let It Begin Here! Lexington & Concord: First Battles of the American Revolution*, published by Walker. The Fradins are currently writing a biography of social worker and anti-war activist Jane Addams for Clarion and a nonfiction book about a slave escape for National Geographic Children's Books. Turning Points in U.S. History is Dennis Fradin's first series for Marshall Cavendish Benchmark. The Fradins have three grown children and three young grandchildren.